42260000191106

W9-AAI-516

Historical Atlases of South Asia,
Central Asia, and the Middle East™

A HISTORICAL ATLAS OF

LEBANON

Carolyn M. Skahill

The Rosen Publishing Group, Inc., New York

Published in 2004 by The Rosen Publishing Group, Inc.
29 East 21st Street, New York, NY 10010

Copyright © 2004 by The Rosen Publishing Group, Inc.

First Edition

All rights reserved. No part of this book may be reproduced in any form without permission in writing from the publisher, except by a reviewer.

Publisher Cataloging Data

Skahill, Carolyn M.
A historical atlas of Lebanon / Carolyn M. Skahill.
    p. cm. — (Historical atlases of South Asia, Central Asia, and the Middle East)
Includes bibliographical references and index.
Summary: Maps and text chronicle the history of this small Middle Eastern country that suffered a civil war period from 1975 to 1991.
ISBN 0-8239-3982-0
1. Lebanon—History—Maps for children 2. Lebanon—Maps for children [1. Lebanon—History 2. Atlases]
I. Title II. Series
911'.5692—dc21

Manufactured in the United States of America

Cover images: The country now known as Lebanon *(present-day map, center)* and its historic city of Beirut *(French twentieth-century map, background)* were once a part of the Eastern Roman Empire under Constantine the Great, pictured on the Roman coin *(bottom left)*, and later a part of the Turkish Ottoman Empire under Selim the Grim *(bottom right)*. Since 1998, Lebanon has been governed by President Emile Lahoud *(top left)*.

Contents

MEDITERRANEAN

SEA

Tripoli

BEIRUT ■

Zahla

Sidon

GOLAN HEIGHTS
territory claimed by Syria
and occupied by Israel

GOLAN

HEIGHTS

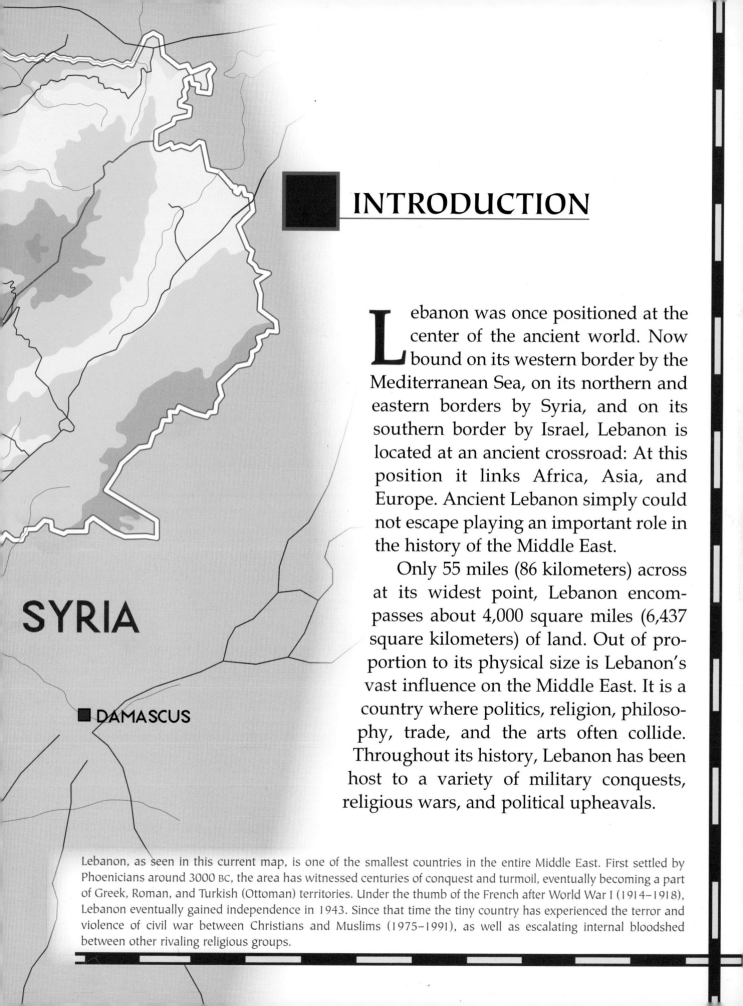

INTRODUCTION

Lebanon was once positioned at the center of the ancient world. Now bound on its western border by the Mediterranean Sea, on its northern and eastern borders by Syria, and on its southern border by Israel, Lebanon is located at an ancient crossroad: At this position it links Africa, Asia, and Europe. Ancient Lebanon simply could not escape playing an important role in the history of the Middle East.

Only 55 miles (86 kilometers) across at its widest point, Lebanon encompasses about 4,000 square miles (6,437 square kilometers) of land. Out of proportion to its physical size is Lebanon's vast influence on the Middle East. It is a country where politics, religion, philosophy, trade, and the arts often collide. Throughout its history, Lebanon has been host to a variety of military conquests, religious wars, and political upheavals.

SYRIA

■ DAMASCUS

Lebanon, as seen in this current map, is one of the smallest countries in the entire Middle East. First settled by Phoenicians around 3000 BC, the area has witnessed centuries of conquest and turmoil, eventually becoming a part of Greek, Roman, and Turkish (Ottoman) territories. Under the thumb of the French after World War I (1914–1918), Lebanon eventually gained independence in 1943. Since that time the tiny country has experienced the terror and violence of civil war between Christians and Muslims (1975–1991), as well as escalating internal bloodshed between other rivaling religious groups.

Neatly stacked on the bottom of the Mediterranean Sea, amphorae from a Phoenician ship are seen in this underwater photograph from the National Geographic Society. At the time of their discovery in 1999, they were a part of an underwater archaeological site believed to be the wreckage of two ancient Phoenician ships that sank off the coast of Israel in 750 BC. Historians believe the ships were transporting wine from Tyre, Lebanon, to ports in Egypt.

Few countries of similar size have amassed such a grand list of historic events, including conquests by Alexander the Great, Emperor Constantine, and Napoleon. The Lebanese people have survived these raids by incorporating conquerors and foreign peoples into their society and absorbing their philosophies, religions, and cultures.

The ancient Lebanese began as maritime traders. The people of ancient Lebanon who traded with Greece were known as Phoenicians, a name given to them by the Greeks and derived from *phoinikies*, the Greek word for "purple." The Phoenicians had created a purple dye from a shellfish called the murex. The murex shell was found on the shores of the Mediterranean, and eventually the purple color it produced became a popular one,

very much in demand. It has been said that Cleopatra was fond of purple and wore it often.

The Phoenicians also brought new ideas into ancient Lebanon, discoveries made during their frequent journeys. Inspired by Egyptian pictorial writing known as hieroglyphics, the Phoenicians created the single most important human innovation—the alphabet, or pictures based on sounds. As this alphabet was introduced, it gave the Greeks the ability to record literature, it allowed the Romans to define their legal heritage, and it enabled Christians, Jews, and Muslims to memorialize their revelations.

As you will discover in this book, modern Lebanon, in part because of its place in the world, is a product of dynamic cultures, religions, and conflicts from its past.

1 ANCIENT LEBANON

Except for a small strip of maritime plain, ancient Lebanon did not lend itself to extensive agriculture and farming. Its land was narrow and much of it was covered by two separate mountain ranges running north to south—the Lebanon Mountains and the Anti-Lebanon Mountains. The Qadisha River runs parallel to the mountains as it did in ancient times. Its source lies north of the western mountain range. Its other end flows near present-day Tripoli, where it spills into the Mediterranean Sea. The ruins of many monasteries and hermitages may still be found along its banks.

The Phoenicians

The first known inhabitants of Lebanon were the Canaanites, a Semitic people with a culture similar to that of the people of Syria and Palestine. The Canaanites eventually traded with the Greeks and were known by them as Phoenicians. They were seagoing merchants living in what were then independent city-states in the eastern Mediterranean. They established colonies throughout the region and along the shores of the Mediterranean Sea. These outposts served as depots for the exchange of goods with Europe in the west and Asia in the east.

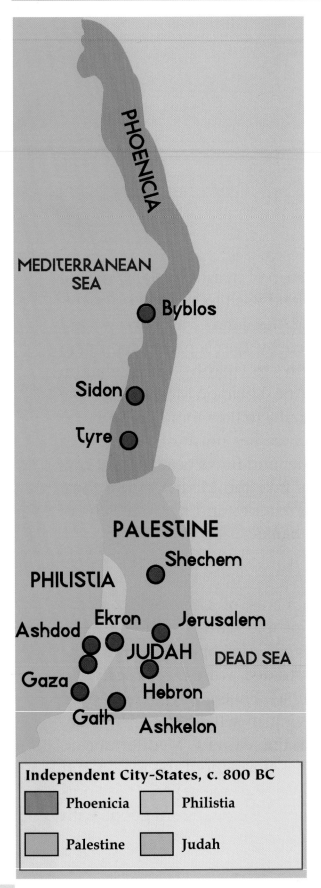

MEDITERRANEAN SEA

PHOENICIA

● Byblos

Sidon ●

Tyre ●

PALESTINE

PHILISTIA

● Shechem

Ekron ● Jerusalem ●

Ashdod ●

● JUDAH

Gaza ● ● DEAD SEA

Gath ● Hebron ●

Ashkelon

Independent City-States, c. 800 BC

Phoenicia   Philistia

Palestine   Judah

The Phoenicians had turned to maritime trade to survive and had become master navigators. To do so, they had studied a form of navigation that relied upon the North Star, or Polaris. The Phoenicians built their ships of cedar, which was plentiful in ancient Lebanon. They sailed to foreign ports all across the Mediterranean and traded excess cedar, olive oil, and wine for gold and other items. They introduced the olive tree to Europe and brought back to Lebanon ivy, laurel, and other plants. They also returned with many innovative ideas gleaned from their distant travels.

The actual recorded history of the country now known as Lebanon began around 3000 BC. By this time, the Phoenicians, who had already been trading with the Egyptians for centuries, developed the first alphabet—pictures based on sounds. The idea had come to them from the hieroglyphics they had seen in Egypt. The Phoenicians are also credited with discovering the formula for glass as well as for a popular shade of purple dye derived from seashells. These innovations, and the increase in trade that resulted from them, motivated the Phoenicians to explore the far reaches of the known world. In the process

This map shows Israelite settlements in Palestine and Judah (illustrated here as it was divided after King Solomon's death in 922 BC), Philistine settlements in Philistia, and Phoenician settlements in Phoenicia.

they introduced to Lebanon many foreign ideas and cultures, and a variety of religious and political beliefs.

Semitic Invaders

The early, pre-Christian millennia in the region were peaceful and productive. Phoenicia had become an extensive trading center, and Phoenicians had established good relationships with Egyptians and Mesopotamians. This tranquility lasted until around 1600 BC, when a nomadic, Semitic (from ancient southwestern Asia) people conquered Egypt. About 100 years later, these Semitic Egyptians invaded the regions now known as Syria and Lebanon and incorporated those territories into Egypt.

These invaders had a less developed culture than the Phoenicians did. After being conquered by the Egyptians, however, the Phoenicians did not regain their independence until the beginning of the twelfth century BC. At this time, trade with other Mediterranean city-states resumed. The Phoenicians further developed their alphabet, crafted textiles, and carved ivory. They also created beautiful and functional wares from glass and imported

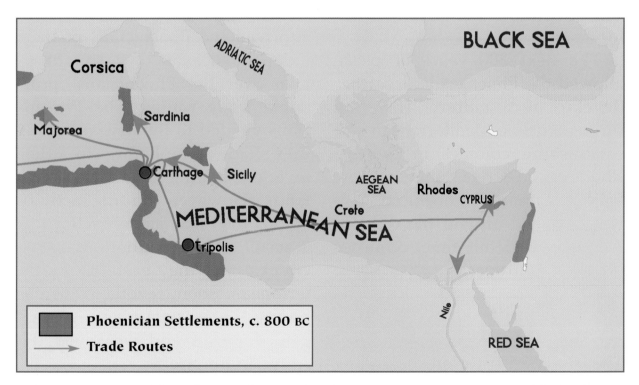

Phoenicians, a peaceful people generally remembered as great sea navigators, often paid high tributes (taxes) to neighboring civilizations in order to increase their ability to trade with foreign cultures. By trading, they spread much of what they had learned to other regions, sharing their beliefs, language, skills, and artistry with Assyrians, Egyptians, Mycenaeans, and Minoans. In fact, it is now largely accepted that Phoenician sailors navigated around the coast of Africa at the end of the ninth century BC, centuries before the European explorers.

Landscape and Climate

Throughout the millennia, the mountains of Lebanon have provided isolation to outcasts from neighboring political systems and nurtured a variety of religious divisions, or sects. Lebanon became a sanctuary. This physical isolation divided its inhabitants, however, enabling each faction to pursue its own beliefs. The numerous ideologies created problems in later history, conflicts that continue into the present day.

The mountains also helped establish diverse flora and fauna. Lebanon is the only land in the Middle East without a desert or a bedouin (nomadic) population.

There are generally two distinct seasons in Lebanon: the rainy season that runs from November through March, and the remaining dry season. The average rainfall in Lebanon's coastal areas is about thirty-three inches (eighty-four centimeters). Generally, the mountains prevent moisture, which comes from winds blowing over the Mediterranean Sea, from traveling farther inland. These are cool winds, not the desert winds that prevail in the rest of the Middle East.

metal, which were also offered for trade.

The next 300 years of peace allowed the Phoenicians to further develop as a culture, traveling throughout the Mediterranean and establishing colonies in Cyprus, Rhodes, and Crete. Scholars now believe that master Phoenician navigators sailed around the coast of Africa around this time, centuries before the Europeans.

Assyrian and Babylonian Rule

The Assyrian invasion, beginning in 875 BC, was similar to the Semitic invasion of centuries before. The Assyrians, with powerful leaders like Tiglath-Pileser III, were tyrannical rulers who deprived the Phoenicians of their independence as they sought to take over the Phoenicians' profitable trade routes. The Phoenicians yielded to the new rulers, as they had done before to other invaders, hoping to trade with new lands. However, trading activity among the Phoenicians declined as a result of competition from the Greeks in the eastern Mediterranean. Soon, revolts by neighboring Mesopotamian groups gained power and weakened the Assyrian Empire.

During the seventh century BC, the Babylonians came to power, beginning the Persian Empire under Cyrus the Great. As a result, the Phoenicians were enslaved. Although they supported Persia during the Greco-Persian Wars (492–479 BC), they were then overburdened by tributes (taxes) imposed by Persian successors. These conflicts were considered the final contest between the two maritime superpowers—the Phoenicians and the Greeks.

The Greeks

In early 334 BC, Alexander the Great, then twenty years of age, led an army of 35,000 soldiers to Asia Minor. One year later, he defeated the Persian Empire and moved into the territory that would later be modern Lebanon. Although Alexander died about a decade later in 323 BC, he did begin to

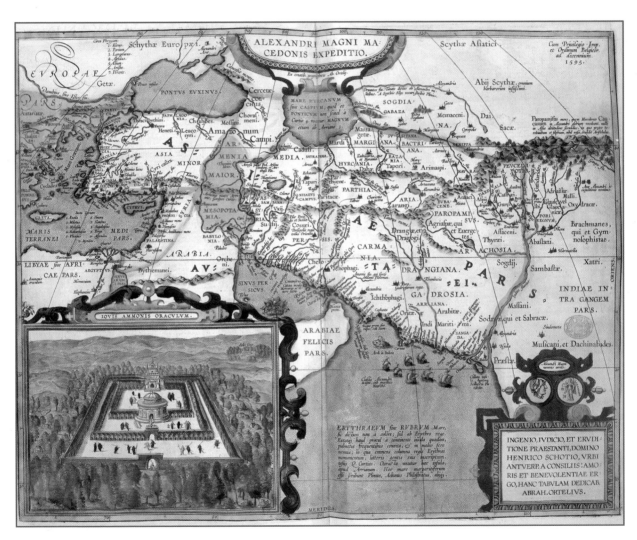

This sixteenth-century map by Flemish cartographer Abraham Ortelius (1527–1598) was a part of the world's first historical atlas. Depicting Alexander the Great's Asian conquests—partly fact, partly fantastic—the image was once featured as a part of Ortelius's book of world maps entitled *Theatrum Orbis Terrarum* (Theatre of the World). The book, the most successful of its time, was published in thirty-one editions and seven different languages between the years of 1570 and 1612 and made Ortelius a wealthy man.

BLACK SEA

MACEDONIA

CASPIAN SEA

MEDITERRANEAN SEA

Tigris

Nineveh

Euphrates

Damascus

Babylon

Susa

Alexandria

Memphis

EGYPT

PERSIAN GULF

ARABIA

Medina

Nile

Mecca

Route of Alexander the Great (334–323 BC)

Macedonian Empire

This map shows the greatest extent of the Macedonian Empire under Alexander the Great. After he had fully defeated the Persians around 330 BC, he exhibited the traits of a dictator and adopted the styles of Persian dress, decisions that greatly annoyed his generals. Alexander died before he could fully unite his empire. The inset map shows how Alexander's territories were divided into kingdoms after his death in 323 BC. His immediate followers, known as the Diadochi, included Antigonus I, Ptolemy I, Seleucus I, and Lysimachus. (The conflicts between them for territory are known as the War of the Diadochi.) Divisions of his empire under Cassander and Chandragupta came later.

Alexandria Eskhata
(Kokard)

Bactra

Alexandria Aeria
(Herat)

Taxila

Alexandria
(Kandahar)

Pasargadae

Persepolis

Pura

The Division of Alexander's Empire Between 306–303 BC

1 Antigonus   4 Ptolemy
2 Seleucus   5 Cassander
3 Lysimachus   6 Chandragupta

Black
Sea

5

3

Byzantium

1

Caspian
Sea

Alexandria Aeria
(Herat)

2

Euphrates

Tigris

Rhodes

Crete

Cyprus

Mediterranean
Sea

Gaza

Babylon

Susa

Persepolis

Alexandria

Memphis

EGYPT

ARABIA

Medina

Persian Gulf

Pura

6

Pattala

Nile

Red Sea

Mecca

Arabian Sea

4

This detail of a mosaic originally found in Pompeii and now located in Naples, Italy, depicts Alexander the Great at the Battle of Issus in which he defeated Darius III and the Persian army in 333 BC. After the defeat, all of Phoenicia became part of Alexander's empire. By the time he reached Egypt one year later in 332, its rulers surrendered without argument. Though it has been said that he was on a mission to conquer the entire Persian Empire, he also had the desire to spread Hellenistic, or Greek, ideas throughout his conquered territories. In doing so, he named many cities Alexandria after himself and introduced the Greek language to Persia.

see the Hellenistic legacy that he left behind in the region. This exchange of cultural ideas between the Mediterranean and the Middle East continues to this day.

After Alexander's death, his huge empire—with territories that spanned through present-day Turkey, Iraq, Iran, Afghanistan, Pakistan, Egypt, and portions of India—was in chaos. Although he had had four strong generals, none had the potential to rule the entire empire. Therefore, it was decided that the empire would be divided into sections, each of which would be ruled by one general independently. Lebanon fell into the eastern portion, which included Phoenicia, Asia Minor, northern Syria, and Mesopotamia. This eastern portion was ruled by General Seleucus and, after his death, by the Seleucid dynasty. When Seleucus's power began to wane, the city-states in Phoenicia—Byblos, Sidon, and Tyre—wanted to become independent. This period of history was filled with disorder and struggle until 64 BC when the Roman general Pompey added Syria and Phoenicia to the Roman Republic.

2 THE ROMAN EMPIRE

In 64 BC, the Roman general Pompey conducted a successful campaign to conquer the Middle East. At this time, Roman rule over the territory that would later be known as Lebanon began. Under the Roman Republic, Phoenicia was incorporated into Syria. Aramaic and Greek soon replaced the Phoenician language. This was a chaotic time among the politicians in Rome, leading to the murder of Julius Caesar, who, at the time of his death in 44 BC, was acting as dictator.

There were many Romans who fought for ultimate authority over the whole of the republic, which was now divided into separate provinces and became known as the Roman Empire. In 27 BC, Augustus Caesar, the adopted son of Julius Caesar, came to power, becoming the first Roman emperor.

The Roman rule established by Augustus Caesar lasted 350 years. It covered the territory from the Atlantic Ocean and the North Sea to the Persian Gulf and the Sahara Desert. Conquering this territory had been the objective of many earlier invaders, but only the Romans actually succeeded.

Pax Romana

This rule by Rome began a period of *Pax Romana*, or Roman peace, in the empire. It was a time of great

This map (*above*), first printed in 1884, illustrates the Roman Empire during the first century after the death of Jesus Christ, or about 400 years before Christianity was the official religion of the empire. Prior to this, Romans were pagans who worshiped a variety of gods and made sacrifices at various temples. Several temples may be seen here, including the Temple of Jupiter, the chief Roman god, and the Temple of Minerva, the goddess of wisdom. Although Emperor Constantine outlawed the persecution of Christians in AD 306, it wasn't until after his death that Christianity largely gained acceptance. Along with the prosperity and growth of the Roman Empire came a system of roadways such as the one shown here (*top right*) that linked the cities of Antioch and Aleppo.

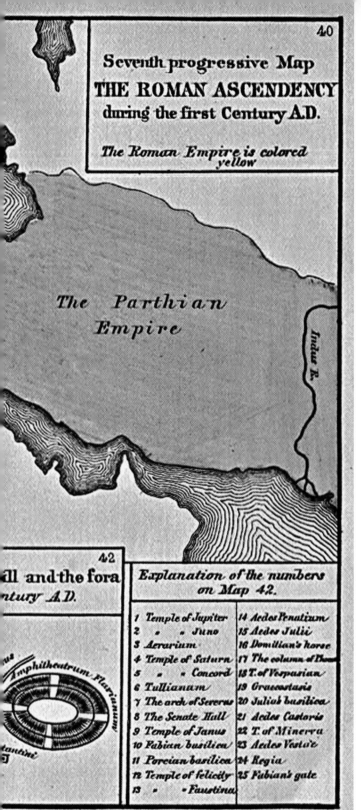

40

Seventh progressive Map
THE ROMAN ASCENDENCY
during the first Century A.D.

The Roman Empire is colored
yellow

The Parthian
Empire

Indus R.

42

ll and the fora
ntury A.D.

Amphitheatrum Flavianum

antini

Explanation of the numbers on Map 42.	
1 Temple of Jupiter	14 Aedes Penatium
2 „ „ Juno	15 Aedes Julii
3 Aerarium	16 Domitian's horse
4 Temple of Saturn	17 The column of Bo...
5 „ „ Concord	18 T. of Vespasian
6 Tullianum	19 Graecostasis
7 The arch of Severus	20 Julius basilica
8 The Senate Hall	21 Aedes Castoris
9 Temple of Janus	22 T. of Minerva
10 Fabian basilica	23 Aedes Vestae
11 Porcian basilica	24 Regia
12 Temple of felicity	25 Fabian's gate
13 „ „ Faustina	

prosperity for the Middle Eastern region. The Romans initiated urban developments such as improved harbors and paved roadways. Temples, baths, and palaces were built or refurbished. Roman roads linked cities to each other for the ease of trading and traveling. For the first time, exporting goods became swift, and outsiders traveled to the Middle East and Europe for pleasure as well as business. The period marked a great cultural exchange between the East and the West.

Merchant centers, such as those located in Byblos, Sidon, and Tyre, began to organize the production of pottery, glass, and purple dye. Cedar, perfume, jewelry, and other products were also produced and distributed using the improved Roman infrastructure. The production of goods became so efficient, in fact, that the Romans built warehouses to store excess goods. The Romans also incorporated the city of Berytus into their empire, and it eventually became the home of a famous school of Roman law. Today, Berytus is Beirut, the capital of modern Lebanon.

Although Augustus was an emperor mostly concerned with peace, the empire did expand under his reign. Before his death, the Roman Empire included territory in present-day Spain, France, and Hungary.

The Birth of Christianity

The persecution of the Christians, which had taken place at the beginning of the fourth century AD, produced many martyrs. Under Emperor Constantine I, also known as Constantine the Great, this religious intolerance was replaced by an acceptance of a variety of religious practices throughout the empire. Constantine, who shared power in Constantinople (Istanbul) at the beginning of his reign in AD 306, was the sole ruler of the region from AD 324 to 327. After his conversion to Christianity in AD 312, he introduced the religion into all of the territory he ruled.

Emperor Constantine ended the persecution of Christians. He is best remembered for making Christianity—one of the world's three most widespread monotheistic religions, along with Judaism and Islam—the official religion of the Roman Empire. Constantine's mother, also a devout Christian, was later elevated by the

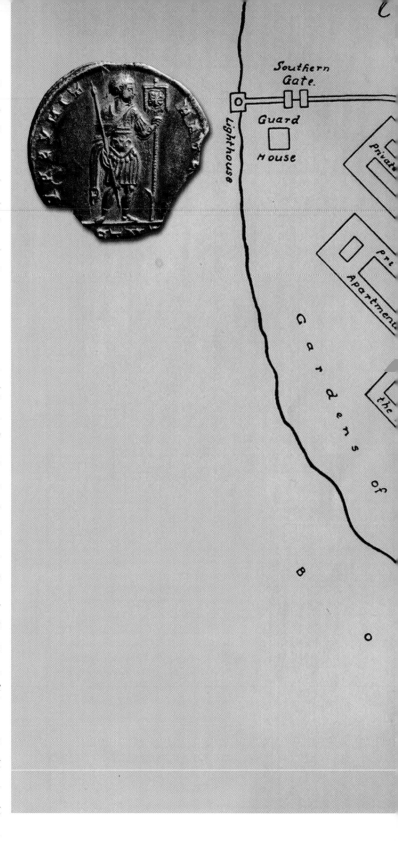

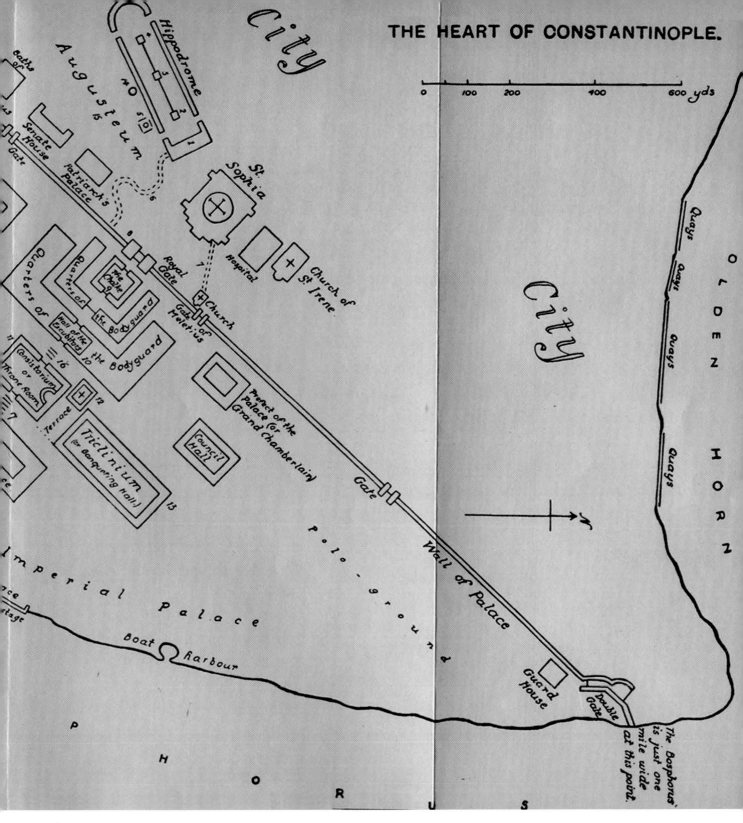

The map shown on these pages, entitled "The Heart of Constantinople," was first printed in *East and West Through Fifteen Centuries*, an atlas printed in 1916. The Roman emperor Constantine I *(pictured on the Roman coin, top left)* founded the city in AD 330 on the site of what was once Byzantium and what is now present-day Istanbul, Turkey. Soon the well-fortified city was the heart of the Eastern Roman Empire. Later the seat of Ottoman (Turkish) power in the fifteenth century, Constantinople was transformed from a Christian city to an Islamic one, and the church of St. Sophia (the present-day Hagia Sophia) was turned into a mosque.

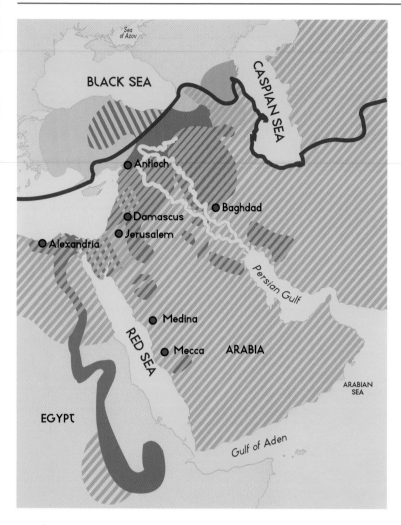

The Spread of Christianity, AD 700–1000

Christian area c. 700

Area converted to Christianity c. 700–1050

Monophysite Christian area c. 700

Nestorian Christian area c. 700

Extent of area under Muslim rule c. 1000

—— Boundary of area under Muslim rule c. 800

church to sainthood. It was she who founded the Church of the Holy Sepulchre on the supposed site of Christ's crucifixion as well as the Church of the Nativity in Bethlehem, both of which still stand.

Christ's apostles likely traveled to and through the region because of its proximity to the Holy Lands. Those who followed Christ's teachings brought with them a strong religious community and built many Christian churches. By the end of the second century AD, there was a Christian bishop in Tyre and many Christians studying in Berytus (Beirut). The academies, including those located in Berytus, became places of study for religious men. This is where Romans studied law, science, philosophy, Greek, and Latin.

The Byzantine Empire

It was Constantine who founded the capital of the eastern empire that bore his name, Constantinople. By the third century AD, the Roman Empire had

This sixth-century mosaic of Jerusalem (AD 565), on the floor of the Church of Madaba in present-day Jordan, shows the Roman architecture of the city during that time, including the divided cardo, the arch of Ecce Homo, and the Neapolis Gate, in addition to other Byzantine structures. Religious images of this sort are almost never seen in floor mosaics since it is considered blasphemous to step upon them.

During the fifth century AD, under Byzantine rule, intellectual life flourished in the region and commercial activity grew. The eastern empire—including present-day Lebanon—came to know a period of prosperity and growth.

Then, during the sixth century AD, everything suddenly changed. The land was ravaged by a series of earthquakes. Coastal cities were immersed in floodwaters, destroying the commercial infrastructure between AD 551 and 555.

The schools in Berytus were in shambles, the temples demolished. Palaces were devastated, and its renowned law school was in ruins. More than 30,000 people were killed in the earthquakes and floods. The fear of divine wrath at this time was such that many nonreligious people now embraced Christianity.

At this same time, there also began a period of corruption in the Roman government. Political abuse by those in power became widespread as leaders began demanding excessive taxes from the people. In addition, Roman leaders were unsuccessful at calming the disorder brought about after the recent devastation. As a result, the empire fell into a weakened state and became easy prey to new conquerors.

split into two parts as a result of infighting and other internal strife: the eastern Byzantine Empire and the Western Roman Empire. The western section kept its capital in Rome, and the eastern portion had its capital in Constantinople (present-day Istanbul). Eastern influence on the empire strengthened as the center of the culture moved, from Rome to Constantinople.

During this time, many temples throughout the empire were converted to Christian churches. Christianity dominated the region. More than fifteen hundred years later, a 1932 census showed that Christians outnumbered all other religious groups in Lebanon.

3 ARAB CONQUEST

Alexandria

EGYPT

Muhammad, the founder of Islam, was born in AD 570 in the city of Mecca, in Arabia. The son of a camel driver, his birth was of little note at the time, but his birthplace later became a destination of pilgrimage for Muslims, or those who practice Islam. In order to lay the foundation for his religious philosophy, Muhammad migrated from Mecca to Medina in AD 622. The year of this migration marks the first year of the Muslim calendar.

Muhammad was said to have had a series of mystical experiences. He received messages throughout his life from the archangel Gabriel. He later recited these words as the religious teachings of Islam. The word "Islam" actually means "submission," in other words, to literally submit to the recited messages, which were later reproduced in the Koran, the Islamic holy book.

Islam, which spread rapidly after the death of Muhammad in AD 632, moved beyond the confines of Arabia to the entire Persian Empire within twenty years. By the ninth, tenth, and eleventh centuries, Islam entered its true golden age, evolving into a brilliant and accomplished culture. Muslims were responsible for translating many important Greek works into Arabic, constructing beautiful works of architecture, advancing the sciences of medicine and astronomy, developing algebra and the concept of zero, and inventing the astrolabe and quadrant.

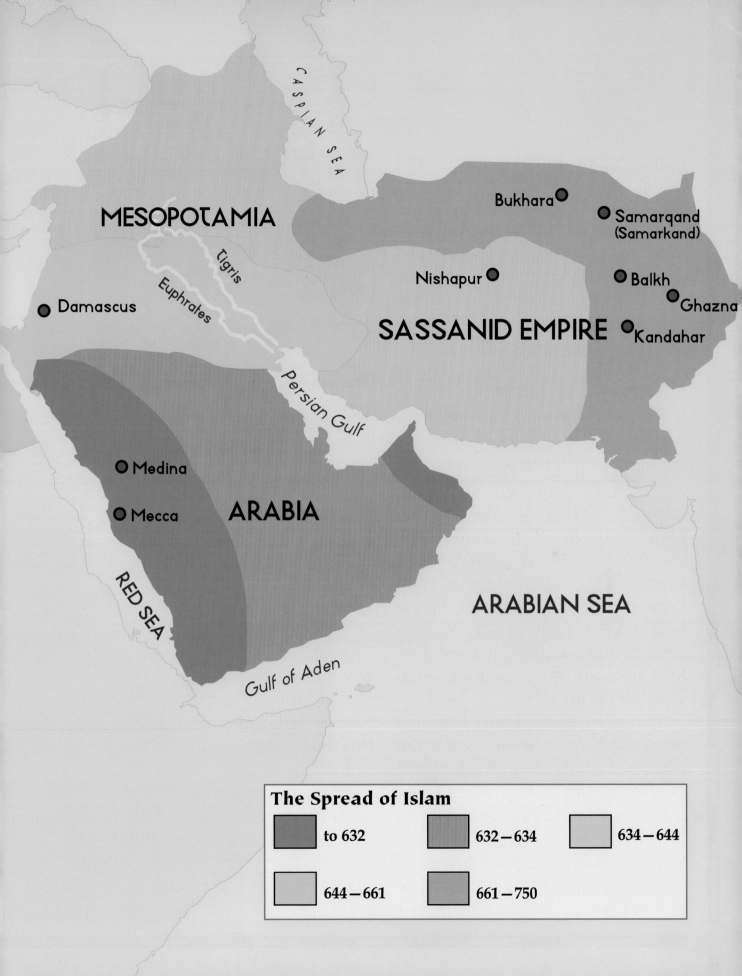

CASPIAN SEA

MESOPOTAMIA

Tigris

Euphrates

Damascus

Bukhara

Samarqand
(Samarkand)

Nishapur

Balkh

Ghazna

SASSANID EMPIRE

Kandahar

Persian Gulf

Medina

Mecca

ARABIA

RED SEA

Gulf of Aden

ARABIAN SEA

The Spread of Islam

■	to 632	■	632 – 634	■	634 – 644
■	644 – 661	■	661 – 750		

The Muslim faith Muhammad preached has, over the centuries since his death, spread across the globe. It is now the faith of hundreds of millions of people throughout the world. The Koran is considered by the faithful to be the direct word of God. It encompasses the subjects of religion, science, and philosophy, and dictates in detail how a Muslim should live his or her life. These guidelines are referred to as the five tenets of Islam.

The Force of Islam

After the death of Muhammad in AD 632, his followers began an attempt to control both religious and civil life from their established base in Arabia to the eastern Mediterranean. This jihad (holy war) against non-Muslims brought Islam into the region of present-day Lebanon, though the strategic position of Lebanon itself was not evident to the caliphs (successors of Muhammad) in distant Medina, who left the area.

Invasions against non-Muslims began with a raid by Arabs near the Dead Sea in AD 633 at the battle of Wadi al-Arabah. Two years later, Damascus and Palestine fell to these Arab invaders from the East. Soon after, the seacoast towns of Tyre and Sidon also fell. The

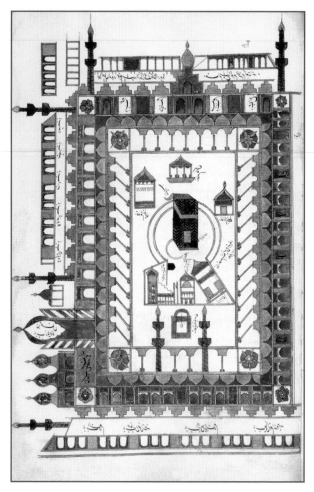

The ka'aba, as seen in this Turkish miniature created in 1620, is located inside the Great Mosque in Mecca. As it was during Muhammad's lifetime, it is the most revered place of worship for Muslims. Muslims from all across the world make pilgrimages to the edifice, which contains a sacred black stone.

Byzantine army, which consisted of 50,000 troops, had fought many battles, but was unable to control this onslaught.

Finally, by AD 637, Muslims overran the entire region. Even the great Persian Empire, which was by then twelve centuries old, could not survive. The Arabs made the inland city Damascus the capital of their conquered states. They were desert people who knew little about maritime trade. Because they also had little interest in farming, they left the coastal towns of Lebanon on their own.

Unlike Lebanon, Persia was dominated by Islam. Persia was positioned inland, and its religious and government institutions were obliterated. The region did not reemerge from the devastation until eight centuries later. This Muslim conquest of the Persian Empire enhanced their deadly reputation and made it easier for them to subdue other lands.

Islamic Dominance

Eventually, the Muslims' goal would be achieved beyond anything they would have thought possible. Christian churches, originally constructed so that the congregation would face toward the east, also fit the Islamic requirement that one must face east when praying—east being the direction of Mecca. By the middle of the second millennium, the Christian frescos in these churches had been completely painted over, and the Christian churches of Constantinople were converted into Islamic mosques. Christianity, which had been brought to the area by Constantine centuries earlier, was obliterated by the Muslim invasion.

Once the battle was over, Muawiya, the founder of the Umayyad dynasty, was appointed the governor of Syria. (Syria, at that time, included Lebanon.) Muawiya ordered Lebanese shipbuilders to construct ships for a navy so that he could fend off any attacks by Byzantine invaders. He also curtailed raids by the Marada, a people living in the Lebanon Mountains who supported Byzantine rule. Finally, Muawiya arranged to pay taxes to the Byzantine rulers in order to stop any future invasions by their supporters.

The Umayyad dynasty's rule continued for another century until about AD 750, when the 'Abbasids, founded by Abul Abbas, invaded the region and conquered Syria and therefore Lebanon. The 'Abbasids were very harsh rulers, and there were many uprisings and rebellions against them by the local peoples.

A Collision of Faiths

At this time, there were a variety of religious groups who repeatedly invaded the region. One after another, these groups were subsequently dominated by some opposing group, a turmoil that has had a lasting impact on current

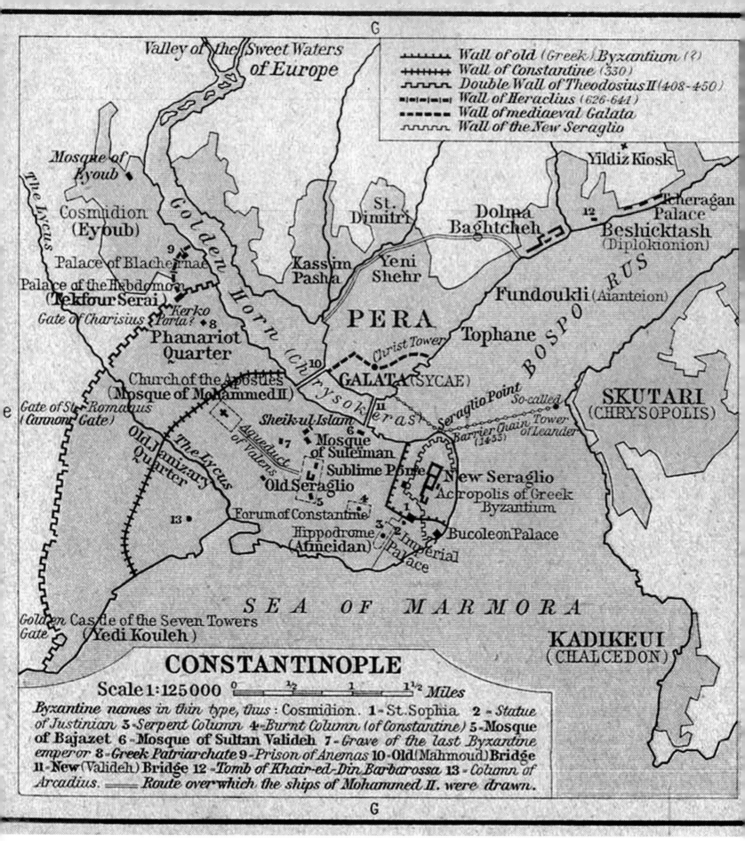

CONSTANTINOPLE

Scale 1:125 000   0   ½   1   1½ *Miles*

Byzantine names in thin type, thus : *Cosmidion*. 1 - *St. Sophia* 2 - *Statue of Justinian* 3 - *Serpent Column* 4 - *Burnt Column (of Constantine)* 5 - *Mosque of Bajazet* 6 - *Mosque of Sultan Valideh* 7 - *Grave of the last Byzantine emperor* 8 - *Greek Patriarchate* 9 - *Prison of Anemas* 10 - *Old (Mahmoud)* **Bridge** 11 - **New** *(Valideh)* **Bridge** 12 - *Tomb of Khair-ed-Din Barbarossa* 13 - *Column of Arcadius.* ——— *Route over which the ships of Mohammed II. were drawn.*

This 1923 map of Constantinople, as William R. Shephard printed it in *The Historical Atlas*, shows the city after it was captured by the Turks and became the seat of Ottoman power. Besides a clear depiction of its various fortifications, some of which date from AD 330, Islamic mosques within the city's walls are also visible. In some cases, as in the Mosque of Mohammad II, Christian churches were modified to become Islamic houses of worship.

Lebanese society. These conflicts eventually left religious communities scattered throughout present-day Lebanon, as well as a variety of Christian sects.

The followers of Saint John Maron, for instance, settled in the northern mountains, while the Jacobites, a rival Christian group, were largely located in Syria. Another Christian group, the Melchites, lived in central Lebanon and followed the decrees of the Council of Chalcedon, the fourth ecumenical council of the Catholic Church. Some Melchite Christians later altered their religious philosophy and became known as Greek Catholics since they used the Greek language.

There was a similar fracturing of the other religions. The Fatimid caliph of Egypt, head of the Fatimid dynasty, claimed a direct descension from Fatima, a daughter of Muhammad. He believed that he was a reincarnation of God. His followers, Hamza and Darazi, developed the dogmas (religious opinions) for this sect. Later, after Darazi left Egypt to spread the new religion, they settled in Lebanon. Followers of the Darazi sect decreed that Jews and Christians could not hold office or ride horses and had to wear black robes.

The Christian, Muslim, and Darazi religions constitute the major religious communities of modern Lebanon. Because of the presence of such diverse religious communities, the Lebanese confessional state emerged as its primary political structure. In this type of governance, the various religious communities are represented in political matters according to their population. In other matters, such as religion, each group is allowed to observe its own laws.

Islam's Golden Age

During the period of Arab rule at the end of the first millennium, there was a resurgence of intellectualism. Universities prospered, the study of literature and philosophy was encouraged, and the physical sciences were rediscovered. There was also economic prosperity as warehouses filled with textiles, glass, and ceramics, and the harbors filled with ships. These wares were sought-after throughout Europe and the Near East.

Although the ethnic and religious groups remained separate, they worked well together for political and commercial purposes. The Arab rulers were tolerant of the various religious sects. They continued the practice of exempting non-Muslims from military service and instead exacted special taxes from these groups.

4 THE CRUSADES

The Crusades were the inspiration of Pope Urban II, who had been installed as pope at Avignon, in the south of France. The goal was to recover the Holy Lands, which had been overrun by Muslims. Pope Urban was outraged by the Arab occupation of Christian holy places in Palestine. He was angered by the Arab destruction of Christian places of worship. In AD 1095, he made a speech in an effort to gain the support of the Byzantine emperor in Constantinople, Alexius I, who was at the time also besieged by the Arabs throughout his empire. The crusaders marched from France and other European cities through Constantinople to the Holy Lands.

After liberating Jerusalem, the crusaders moved toward the Lebanese coastline and captured Tripoli, Berytus, and Sidon. In Berytus, the

The map of the Crusades era shows territories gained by crusaders between the eleventh and fourteenth centuries. Christianity itself had largely taken hold in Lebanon by the fourth century. At the beginning of the Christian era, theological differences among the faithful, as well as a landscape crisscrossed by rivers and mountains, allowed for the seclusion of numerous religious sects. Lebanon soon became a destination for a variety of religious minorities who were fleeing persecution elsewhere. This map was first published in the *Public Schools Historical Atlas* in 1905.

General Map
for the
ERA OF THE CRUSADES

Longmans, Green & Co., London, New York & Bombay.

inhabitants gave the invaders provisions in order to spare the city. In other parts of the region, they encountered little resistance. The first initiative of the victorious crusaders was to bring order and control to the region. In order to achieve this, they solicited the cooperation of rulers from all parts of Europe. Crusaders were furnished with replenished recruits, fresh food, and most other supplies required by any large army.

Within two years, by AD 1099, the Christian crusaders had liberated both Asia Minor and Antioch from Arab rule, controlling each region with the help of successful leaders of past campaigns.

By AD 1118, the entire coastal region was effectively under Christian control. Future success in maintaining this Christian dominance in the face of Islam depended greatly on European support. The Christians effectively fortified the lands they had captured, protecting strategic areas by building fortresses and walls, many of which still stand today. These fortifications guarded territory captured from the Muslims against intrusion by Arab peoples east of the Holy Lands and in other territories that were not part of the Frankish Empire.

This medieval manuscript depicts the siege of the city of Antioch by Christian crusaders during the First Crusade in AD 1098. Part of a historical work entitled *The History of Deeds Done Beyond the Sea*, it was written by William of Tyre (1130–1185), a Christian historian and scholar.

The Crusades continued until the fall of Acre in AD 1291. Although Islam reestablished itself in Lebanon, the crusaders left a permanent imprint on the region.

Muslim Rebellion

There was a slow reaction to the invasion of the crusaders. The first to move against them was Zangi, the son of a Turkish slave. He entered Frank-held territories and began to capture a string of cities away from Christian rule, including Edessa in AD 1144.

After Zangi's death, his son Nureddin succeeded him in 1145 and managed to retake Damascus, the capital in Syria, as well as parts of Jordan. The purpose was to include Egypt in the territory. To that end, he sent a general of his army on a mission to Cairo. A nephew of the general's, Saladin, was with this group headed to Egypt. Saladin's goal was to unite the Egyptian Shiite Muslims with the Syrian Sunni Muslims and then to engage in jihad with the crusaders. In AD 1190, he fought the "infidels" and recaptured most of the territory of Lebanon. Still, he did not succeed in uniting Shiite and Sunni Muslims.

That same year, the rulers of Germany, Brittania (England), and France launched a counterattack against Saladin in order to force the Muslims out. In 1192, there was a final battle between the East and the West. In the end, a peace treaty was signed designating that territory from Tyre to the east and south would be Christian-ruled, and Muslim leaders would control the interior, including Syria. This treaty—the beginning of many conflicts in the holy region—partitioned Palestine in a manner similar to one drafted many years later in 1948.

After Saladin died, the territory of Egypt and Syria was split among his sons and brothers, and it eventually fell into decline. Although the Frankish territory was consistently reinforced with European leaders and supplies, the Islamic region had declined and was ripe for invasion by Turkish and Mongolian slaves.

Originally, Egyptian caliphs imported slaves, called Mamluks, from conquered territories in Turkey and Mongolia. The Egyptians educated and controlled these slaves for many years until the thirteenth century. After years of slavery, Mongols came in wave after wave across Asia to the Middle East, slaughtering everything in their path.

Baybars, an Asian-born Mamluk slave and later a general in the Egyptian army, set out to defeat the Mongol forces near Jaffa. Later his son, Baraka, and grandson, Salamish, continued his quest to push back the crusaders. By AD 1291, Salamish succeeded. Knights and foot soldiers were annihilated in the battle at Akka, the definitive end of the conflict between Christianity in the West and Islam in the East.

The centuries that followed brought a period of both natural and man-made disasters to the region. Earthquakes, pillaging, slaughter, and raids were commonplace. In AD 1381, Sidon was attacked and Berytus was sacked and destroyed.

وعارض وصوفيه والسري وغمز على سطح خط الميدان حتى يصلوا الى سط الموكب
شرفتناول العنان مع الدرفة بشماله و يضرب بقائم السيف قبة الدرفة وشي عليها
بالإزايه ونزد فريكك بيناودورق بالدرفه بيشاء عن كل الغرين و يرجع على خط الدابس

الكبير ويجى الخلفه يفعل كفعل الاول وبرد فرسته شما الاعلى خط الدابخ الكبير
ويجى التالت يفعل كفعله صاحبه وبرد فرسته يمناو يجى الاول يفعل كفعل كل فعل ولا درق

This fifteenth-century Arabian illumination, now housed in the Bibliotheque Nationale in Paris, France, depicts Mamluk slaves. The warriors became influential Muslim rulers, dominating the region for some 700 years. Mamluks defeated the last Christian crusaders and stopped Mongol forces from invading Syria in 1260. By the end of the fifteenth century however, the stronger Ottoman forces ended Mamluk rule.

By AD 1404, what was left of Berytus was then set on fire. People began to understand that they would reap more benefits from cooperation than from war.

This realization began a period of peace and expanding commercial activity in the region. In spite of the centuries-long conflicts and relative periods of peace, however, neither the East nor the West gained much insight into one another. Muslims believed Europeans were an inferior race, and the Europeans, while adapting to some local customs, never fully comprehended the Lebanese people. This resistance was further complicated by differences in language and religion. Later in the Middle Ages, instead of war, Christians used the ministry to attempt to persuade Muslims to embrace Christianity.

5 THE OTTOMAN TURKS

The caliphs of Egypt, who ruled in the region of Lebanon, had begun a downward spiral at the beginning of the twelfth century. This was about the same time that the Ottomans emerged in Turkey. Originally central Asian slaves from Turkmenistan, the Ottoman Turks first defeated the Persians and then conquered the Mamluks of Egypt. This period of disorganization in the Middle East contributed to a decline in its trade and commerce.

The Mongols, a nomadic people who had infiltrated central Asia and the Middle East during several centuries of conflict, joined the Turks in their effort to extend their empire. In addition to the Mongols, peoples from Greece, Romania, Bulgaria, and Iraq had also joined the fray by the sixteenth century. Together with the Turks, this group overran parts of Europe and Asia, including present-day Lebanon, Syria, Jordan, and Israel, a region that was at that time known as Greater Syria. Finally, they conquered Constantinople in 1453, the seat of Byzantine power.

Lebanon's sympathies were divided between the Ottoman Turks and the Egyptian Mamluks. The largely Christian population of Berytus maintained their relationship with the Mamluks, while people living in the south joined the Ottomans in their fight against the Egyptians. The Ottomans had earlier claimed their

TURCICI IMPERII IMAGO.

Philip De Bay created this map of the Ottoman Empire in 1630 during one of the calmest stretches in Lebanon's political history. Although the Turkish powers had dominated Lebanon by 1516, the years following the civil war of 1860 were among the country's most peaceful periods. The Turks remained powerful until after World War I, when the French mandated control of Greater Lebanon in 1920.

allegiance to Islam and adopted much of its culture and political institutions, so the population of southern Lebanon became largely Muslim.

By the early part of the sixteenth century, the Ottomans succeeded in controlling the region. When the Turks entered Damascus, Lebanese leaders sent a delegation to pay tribute to Selim I (ruled 1512–1520), the new Ottoman ruler. Selim was impressed by the group that arrived from Lebanon, as well as by their leader, Emir Fakhr ad-Din I (ruled 1516–1544), who was an educated and persuasive person. Fakhr quickly convinced Selim of the loyalty of the Lebanese people.

Selim declared that the region would be allowed to maintain its territory and its authority. The Ottomans—less concerned about Lebanon, then a part of Greater Syria—had many more pressing and urgent problems controlling territory in Persia and Egypt.

Selim was willing to allow powerful ruling families such as the Maans and the Shihabs to rule in Lebanon. The Maans family adopted Druism as their religion while the Shihabs remained faithful to Islam. While the ruling families were in place, Lebanon was prosperous and gained security. Ships from European cities such as Florence, Marseilles, and Venice entered Lebanon and then loaded local goods for export back to European ports.

These activities were quite different from the treatment received by the people of other Ottoman-conquered lands. The people of Ottoman-controlled Syria and Greece, for example, were subjected to the absolute power of the Turks. They were not allowed to hold government or military positions. Their children, often paid to the Turks as tribute, became Ottoman-owned slaves. Finally, Christians living in Syria and Greece were forced to accept Islam as their religion.

Lebanon, on the other hand, was allowed to use its authority to run its government and enact its treaties with foreign powers. Lebanese tributes paid to the Ottomans were not excessive, and the Lebanese were permitted to levy their own taxes. This money fortified improvements

During the Ottoman Empire, a sultan-caliph would control the provinces from his palace in Constantinople. Although a sultan-caliph lived among the intrigues of his harem and was guarded by slaves, he controlled his empire completely. The Ottomans had an elaborate system of rule in the territories. The hierarchy began with several categories of professionals in charge: the military was the first, then the clerics or religious people, and finally the muftis, who were the judges and interpreters of Islamic law. Selim, also known as Yavuz ("the Grim"), who ruled from 1512 to 1520, is shown in this sixteenth-century painting (right) now housed in the Topkapi Palace Museum in Istanbul, Turkey.

in Lebanese infrastructure and government.

The chaos that overran the Middle East at the time of the Ottoman conquests did not particularly affect Lebanon. Its people carried on their traditional way of life.

Because it was believed that Muslim laws were too sacred to be applied to non-believers, the Ottomans assigned non-Muslims to a religious community called a millet, according to their beliefs and not according to their race.

As a result of this categorization, one millet leader decided matters concerning personal relations, including marriage, inheritance problems, and other family issues.

The Empire Weakens

By 1529, the Ottoman Empire, after its siege of Vienna, Austria, came to encompass new territory. The empire now extended from Persia (Iran) to Hungary and from the Balkans to Morocco. The inhabitants of the region, as well as their captors, subscribed to different religious beliefs, spoke a variety of languages, and were unified by no central idea. The only benefit to the Ottoman authorities in Constantinople for maintaining such a diverse group as a single empire was the total collection of its taxes. Eventually, by the nineteenth century, the empire began to self-destruct.

There were many problems at the palace of the sultan-caliph in Constantinople. It was not uncommon for a sultan to murder one or more of his sons to assure a favorite wife that her son would succeed him on the throne. Corruption was commonplace. By 1683, Vienna, the last region to fall to the Turks, was the first to throw off the stronghold

A photograph of Fakhr ad-Din's seventeenth-century castle, which is located in present-day Palmyra, Syria. Although the Druze leader eventually united Berytus (Beirut), Baalbeck, Tyre, Sidon, Acre, Haifa, and Banias, in 1613 he withdrew into exile in Italy when faced with a potential conflict from stronger Ottoman forces.

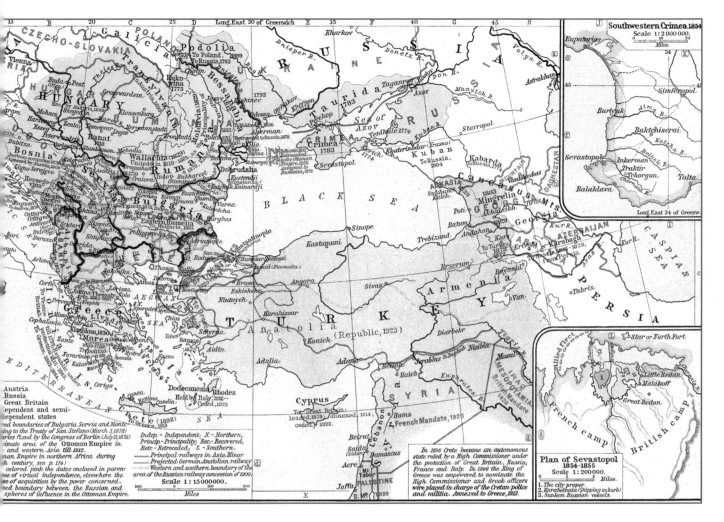

This 1923 map, taken from *The Historical Atlas* by William R. Shephard, shows the decline of the Ottoman Empire. Apparently drawn to indicate changes that occurred around 1910, territory changes in 1913 are shown in dark blue, and changes in 1920–1922 are shown in red. A dashed diagonal line indicates areas that were demilitarized by the 1923 Treaty of Lausanne.

of the Ottoman Empire. By the mid-nineteenth century, the empire had become weak. By the end of that century it had practically expired.

The Turks tried to appease their subjects by improving conditions, but they were unsuccessful. In 1868, the European powers, including Turkey, signed an agreement guaranteeing the authority of Lebanon to self-govern and the continuation of its confessional state. Lebanon was then divided into seven districts, each one governed by a deputy determined by the religious community in each district. This agreement remained the governing document right up to World War I in 1914.

BLACK

REPUBL

CYPRUS
LEBANON
Beirut 1920
PALESTINE

EGYPT

6 WORLD WAR I AND THE CONSTITUTION

By the end of the Ottoman Empire, Lebanon began to change. People looked outward, focusing on the larger world, and expected more freedoms. Unlike other countries in the Middle East, there was already a connection between Lebanon and the West. Trade between Lebanon and Europe was well established. Lebanon also harbored a large Christian population with strong ties to the Vatican. And young Lebanese began to emigrate to the West where they found education and work.

Until the twentieth century, there were in Lebanon, as in most of the Middle East, large class divisions. The population of Lebanon was either distinctly wealthy or very poor. With the increase in education and with more children now able to study, those entering professional positions emerged as a third class of middle-income people.

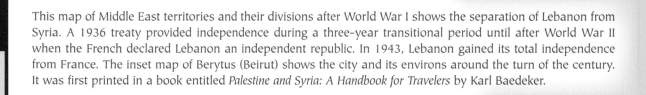

This map of Middle East territories and their divisions after World War I shows the separation of Lebanon from Syria. A 1936 treaty provided independence during a three-year transitional period until after World War II when the French declared Lebanon an independent republic. In 1943, Lebanon gained its total independence from France. The inset map of Berytus (Beirut) shows the city and its environs around the turn of the century. It was first printed in a book entitled *Palestine and Syria: A Handbook for Travelers* by Karl Baedeker.

Knowledge and education among this newly emerged middle class inspired political independence. The Arab population in Lebanon began to assert itself. Arab nationalism was born and the idea of government reform emerged.

Ottoman Control Returns

The Ottomans of Turkey began to clamp down on Lebanon's government administration during World War I (1914–1918). Soon the Ottomans abolished Lebanese authority. The Turkish governor of Syria, Jamal Pasha, who was also charged with overseeing Lebanon, instituted a military seizure of its court system. Many liberal thinkers in Lebanon who sympathized with Western ideas were killed while others sought exile. Lebanon suffered a dark period of oppression during this era, and large portions of its population were exterminated.

Jamal Pasha, known as the Butcher, was commander of Turkish forces in Syria and forced a blockade of the Suez Canal. This order came after his unsuccessful attack on British forces that were protecting it. The blockade stopped supplies from reaching the rival Allied powers (France, Great Britain, Russia, Italy, Japan, and, from 1917, the United States). It also shut down all the ports

of Lebanon and caused famine throughout the region. Soon illness spread without medicine to control it. Under these restrictions, Lebanon suffered more than any other Ottoman province.

San Remo Conference

Assistance finally came at the end of the war in 1918. British forces under General Edmund Allenby and Arab forces led by Faysal I, the son of Sharif Husayn of Mecca, then entered Palestine. Soon Syria and Lebanon were occupied.

In April 1920, at the San Remo Conference in Italy, the Allied powers decided that Lebanon would be put under the jurisdiction of the French. The French government soon appointed General Henri Gouraud to implement the new mandate. Certain territories were considered too poorly established to function independently as nations. These areas, such as Greater Syria (Lebanon, Syria, Jordan, and Israel), Palestine, and Iraq were to be temporarily governed by the Allied powers.

French control over Lebanon was expanded to include Syria, and, at the same time, Great Britain was given jurisdiction over Palestine and Iraq. Soon after, Ottoman rulers in Turkey signed the Treaty of Sevres, renouncing any jurisdiction they

This photograph, taken in 1920 during the San Remo Peace Conference in San Remo, Italy, depicts French commander in chief Marshal Foch, who led the Allied armies in the last stages of World War I, securing their victory. General Badoglio of the Italian Army Corps is also pictured.

had over the region and affirming the new 1920 mandate.

New Borders

The French established Greater Lebanon and redrew its borders to include territory that had earlier been attached to Syria. These boundaries reflect Lebanon's present-day borders and established Berytus, now known as Beirut, as its capital. This created new stresses on the people. Prior to the French mandate, the population was overwhelmingly Christian and educated; after the mandated lands were annexed, Lebanon grew to include a largely less educated Arab population.

In 1926, Lebanon announced the formation of a republic. Its administration drafted a constitution that did not enforce any national religion. The Republic of Lebanon became a confessional republic, which meant

At the conclusion of World War I, Lebanon was governed under a French mandate. During that period, the French redrew its borders and created the Republic of Lebanon, including the Muslim-inhabited coastal plain along with the Christian-dominated mountainous regions. Lebanon remained under French rule until 1943, when it declared its independence.

that its various religious groups were required by law to be represented in government. The number of representatives from each religion who made up Lebanon's Parliament depended upon each religions' percentage of the Lebanese population. Jurisdiction over personal matters belonged to each religious community.

The constitution closely followed the French model. It provided for freedom of assembly and association, as well as for freedom of speech. It allowed for a Chamber of Deputies, a Council of Ministers, and a president to serve for a six-year term. Since the parliamentary offices were divided according to religious lines, a census was taken in 1932. These figures determined the population of the republic and the percentage of each of its religious groups. The same amounts would then determine that group's appropriate representation in Parliament.

Competing for Control

The first president of Lebanon, Charles Dabbas, was Greek Orthodox. At the end of his term in 1932, Bishara al-Khuri and Emile Iddi—both Muslims—competed for the same position. At that time, Henri Ponsot, the French high commissioner, still had absolute control over the government. In 1932, he suspended Lebanon's constitution. At that time, Dabbas's term was extended by one year, preventing any Muslim from entering the office of president. Because French authorities were concerned by Ponsot's actions, Comte Damien de Martel, who appointed Habib as-Saad as president, replaced him. By 1936, President Emile Iddi was elected, and Lebanon's 1926 constitution was reestablished. Within three years, however, it would be suspended again, at the beginning of World War II in 1939.

World War II

In 1941, during World War II, the French government in Vichy took control of Lebanon and appointed General Henri-Fernand Dentz its high commissioner. This appointment led to the resignation of president Iddi. Within months of the appointment, the British overran Lebanon and Syria. Unable to stop the invasion, and after a visit from General Charles de Gaulle, General Dentz resigned, effectively ending Lebanon's Vichy government. As of July 14, the Acre Armistice was in place and the control of Lebanon by the Vichy government was officially over.

After the change in high commissioners, the Lebanese government requested—along with international support—that the French end their mandated control of the country. By 1941, Lebanon officially declared its independence. Although many countries now recognized Lebanon as an independent nation, the French did not abandon it completely until 1943.

By declaring themselves independent, the Lebanese people were now responsible for their own future under delegate General Georges Catroux. Lebanon became a member of both the United Nations and the League of Arab States in 1945.

7 INDEPENDENT LEBANON

LEBANON
French mandate 1920– 194.
Republic 1943 ———
(civil war 1975– 1991)

Although Lebanon was an independent nation by 1941, the country encountered new political, social, and religious issues. Many political factions started separate parties to promote their own, individual political agendas. The Syrian Popular Party, for example, promoted union with Syria, a nation that had lost land after post-war borders were established.

The central government sought to unite the people, asking them to pledge their allegiance to the new nation of Lebanon rather than to any religious faction. The government also continued to follow a policy of collaboration with other Arab countries, while at the same time continuing its longstanding ties with Europe and the West.

Religious Conflicts Continue

The conflict between Christians, who leaned toward the West in their social agendas, and

Suez

Since Lebanon's independence in 1943 and the withdrawal of French troops three years later, its history and politics have been largely shaped by its leaders. Shaken by a violent civil war (1975–1991) between Christians and Muslims over government representation and the influence of the nearly continuous fighting between Israeli and Palestinian forces, Lebanon continues to forge ahead despite instability. This map, which illustrates Lebanon's placement within the Middle East since 1945, shows disputed boundaries as well as oil pipelines.

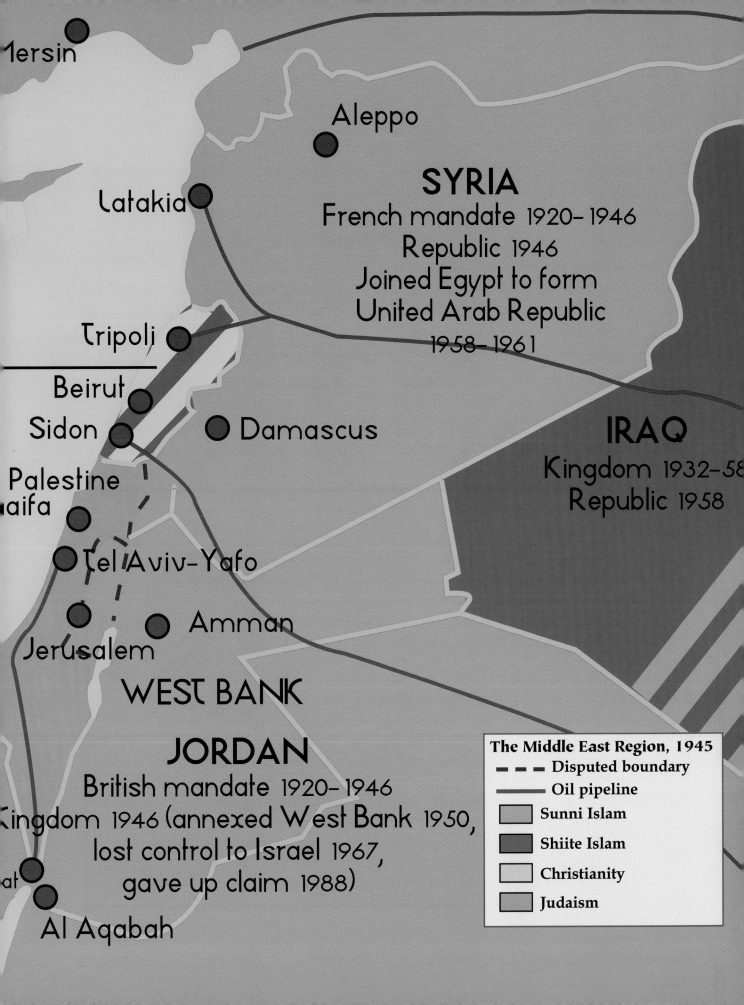

Mersin

Aleppo

SYRIA
French mandate 1920–1946
Republic 1946
Joined Egypt to form
United Arab Republic
1958–1961

Latakia

Tripoli

Beirut

Sidon

Damascus

IRAQ
Kingdom 1932–58
Republic 1958

Palestine

aifa

Tel Aviv-Yafo

Amman

Jerusalem

WEST BANK

JORDAN
British mandate 1920–1946
Kingdom 1946 (annexed West Bank 1950,
lost control to Israel 1967,
gave up claim 1988)

at

Al Aqabah

The Middle East Region, 1945
- - - Disputed boundary
───── Oil pipeline
Sunni Islam
Shiite Islam
Christianity
Judaism

Muslims, who preferred to identify with the Arab world, remained. Problems included issues underlying the fundamental culture of the nation. Christians viewed Arab culture, literature, and education as inferior, and the Muslims insisted that their beliefs be emphasized over Christian ideals.

The first president elected in Lebanon after its independence from the French in 1943 was Bishara al-Khuri. He was reelected for a second term in 1949. After this second election, however, his followers became disillusioned with his increasingly dictatorial manner. Lebanon's religious framework of government was also in question. The Rosewater Revolution, a massive nonviolent rally of more than 50,000 people that took place in 1952, was an organized protest against al-Khuri, who soon resigned.

The Chamber of Deputies next elected Camille Shamun as president. He was a popular leader, although there was substantial criticism that he did not achieve the goals he was elected to pursue, such as balancing Lebanon's religious communities. There was also discontent in the Muslim population, which largely felt that the current administration did not include an appropriate number of

Palestine Liberation Organization

The Palestine Liberation Organization (PLO) is a collective of various guerrilla groups and political factions that was founded in 1964 at the first Arab summit meeting. Led by Yasser Arafat since 1968, the PLO was formed to dissolve the state of Israel, land its members believed rightly belonged to Palestinians. To this end, the PLO had launched numerous attacks against Israel from various countries in the Middle East, including Lebanon. In 1982, the PLO renounced terrorism and recognized Israel's right to exist. By 1993, peace agreements between the PLO and Israel had led them to recognize the need for an independent Palestinian state. Within two years, it was decided that some territories in the West Bank and Gaza Strip should be open to Palestinian rule. These areas included all major Arab cities in the West Bank, except East Jerusalem, territory that has increased slightly in the 1990s. Arafat, now president of the Palestinian-controlled territories, has since revoked the PLO's original charter that called for a dissolution of Israel. The uprisings on both sides, however—with Israelis and Palestinians—have increased over the last few years, resulting in intensifying violence and mounting death tolls.

Muslims in positions of power. They believed that Lebanon's Muslim population outnumbered its Christian population and therefore, according to the constitution, Muslims should hold the highest offices.

Muslims demanded a new census be taken to determine an actual Lebanese religious majority. Christians, however, responded that their constituents included the majority of Lebanon's taxpayers and therefore should retain their government positions. Christians also insisted that immigrants be counted since they were confident that immigrants were largely Christian. The conflict between the two faces of Lebanon—one Christian and one Muslim—grew.

The Rise of Arab Nationalism

When the president of Egypt, Gamal Abdul Nasser, closed the Suez Canal to European traffic in 1956, he caused a crisis. This became a rallying point for Muslims everywhere, including Lebanon. At the same time, Christians believed that maintaining their ties to the West was the only way that Lebanon could hope to retain its independence. Pro-Nasser demonstrations in Lebanon fueled emotions that were already tense.

In 1958, when the entire royal family of Iraq was overthrown and then murdered, many Muslim-controlled areas of Lebanon celebrated. They predicted that the partisan Christian government of Lebanon would be the next to fall. President Shamun invoked articles of the Eisenhower Doctrine. This document obliged the United States military to step in if any Communist-controlled government intervened in a Middle East country and that country requested assistance. Arab nationalism grew.

The United States dispatched troops to the area, fulfilling its obligations in the Middle East under the doctrine, as well as protecting its own regional interests. U.S.-led military forces limited their involvement to a symbolic presence and did not take an active role in the Lebanese civil war. The riots and strikes, which had begun in 1958, quickly escalated to chaos, resulting in the loss of between 2,000 and 4,000 lives. Soon the Chamber of Deputies elected General Fuad Shihab as its new president. Shihab then asked the United States to remove its troops from Lebanon, a request that was quickly granted.

Shihab increased the membership of the Chamber of Deputies from sixty-six to ninety-nine members. This change allowed many of those involved in the revolution to instead become members of the government. During Shihab's presidency, he concentrated on improving Lebanon's infrastructure, providing electricity and clean water to its most remote districts, building medical facilities, and improving the lives of the citizens. Shihab also continued the practice of following a neutral foreign policy. He promoted hospitable relations with neighboring Arab nations and maintained important contacts with the West.

Smoke rises from the shattered wreckage of a department store after the explosion of a bomb in downtown Beirut in this photograph taken on July 8, 1958. Scores of people were injured by the bomb, which was planted by a terrorist group.

Lebanese soldiers stand guard in Beirut in front of a billboard with images of the late Syrian president Hafez al-Assad and his two sons, the current president Bashar al-Assad (*right*), and Basil al-Assad (*left*) as Arab summit delegates leave Lebanon in 2002. The summit was organized to propose peace talks between Arab nations and Israel in return for the Jewish state's exit from territory captured in the 1967 Arab-Israeli war.

In 1964, when elections were held, Charles Hilu succeeded President Shihab. An intellectual and an experienced diplomat, Hilu promoted Lebanon as an independent nation and attempted to ease the tensions between political factions in the region.

Tensions Mount

These attempts were, however, interrupted by the Arab-Israeli war that took place in 1967. This event greatly increased tensions between Christians and Muslims in Lebanon and throughout the Middle East. It also compounded the conflicts by introducing into Lebanon a growing number of Palestinian guerrillas. The Palestinians' intent was to use the southern region of Lebanon as a base from which to launch attacks against Israel.

In 1970, a Christian from the north, Suleiman Franjiyah, was elected president. He had little

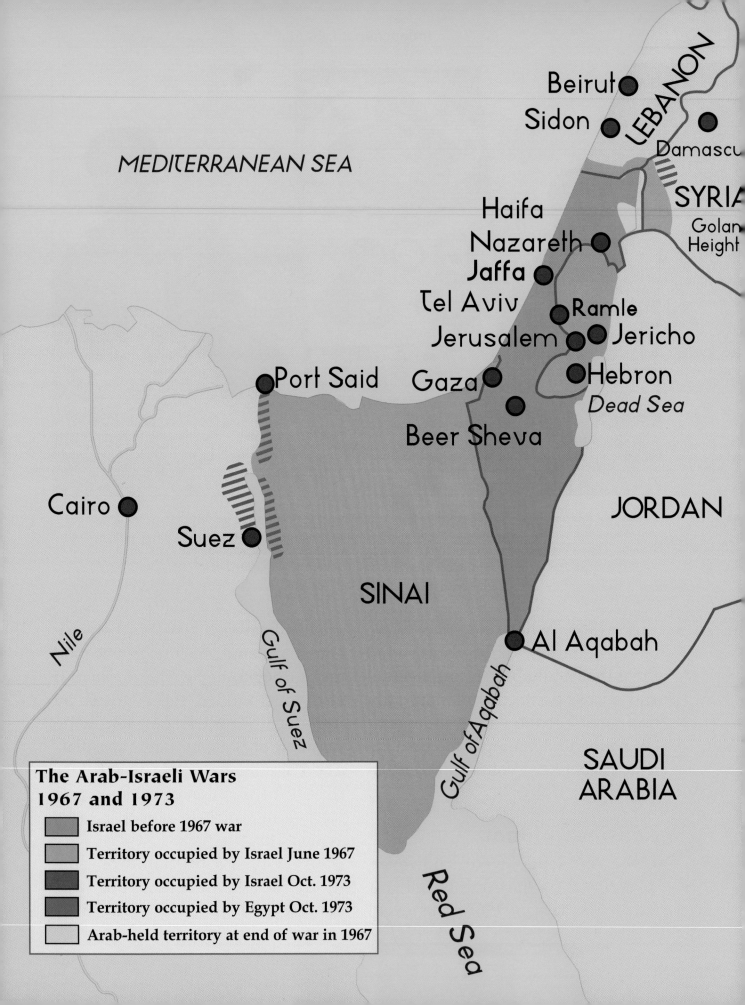

MEDITERRANEAN SEA

Beirut
Sidon
LEBANON
Damascu
SYRIA
Golan
Height

Haifa
Nazareth
Jaffa
Tel Aviv
Ramle
Jerusalem
Jericho
Port Said
Gaza
Hebron
Dead Sea
Beer Sheva

Cairo
JORDAN
Suez
Nile
Gulf of Suez
SINAI
Al Aqabah
Gulf of Aqabah
SAUDI
ARABIA

Red Sea

The Arab-Israeli Wars
1967 and 1973

Israel before 1967 war

Territory occupied by Israel June 1967

Territory occupied by Israel Oct. 1973

Territory occupied by Egypt Oct. 1973

Arab-held territory at end of war in 1967

The Arab-Israeli wars were fought between Israel and the Arab states of Egypt, Syria, Jordan, and Iraq. In the Six-Day War, Israel gained territories such as the Golan Heights and areas around the Suez Canal, as shown on this map *(left)*. In the Yom Kippur War, Israeli forces were pushed back from the Suez Canal after a surprise attack. Both conflicts led to the signing of the Camp David Accords. A grieving mother of a slain Israeli athlete is restrained *(right)* during her son's funeral services in Munich, Germany, in 1972. Her son was among eleven Israeli athletes murdered by Palestinian terrorists.

leadership experience and was the choice of those who preferred a weaker role for the president. That same year, large numbers of Palestinian guerrillas were expelled from Jordan and moved into Lebanon, where there were even more violent clashes between opposing groups.

The Israelis considered any attack on an Israeli citizen, wherever it occurred, as a direct attack on the nation of Israel. Any attack on an Israeli would be met with counterattack. When Palestinians entered the Olympic Village in Munich in 1972 and killed eleven Israeli athletes they were holding captive, Israel countered with a retaliatory incursion (hostile entry) into the Palestinian guerrilla–controlled area in southern Lebanon. This Israeli-led raid on Beirut in 1973 resulted in the deaths of three leaders of the Palestinian Resistance Movement. Violence quickly spread to other parts of the country, and the PLO presence in Lebanon increased.

Though attempts were made at the political level to limit guerrila activity in Lebanon, soon the Israeli-Arab conflict (October 1973 war) overrode any policies of non-violence. Lebanon, unable to resolve the conflict, fell further into chaos. By 1975, that chaos erupted into a civil war of Christians versus Muslims, though the infighting between the Lebanese was actually far more complex.

8 MODERN LEBANON

The nature of Lebanon was changing. Even the traditional style of Lebanese homes were being replaced with Western-style, boxy apartment buildings. Jobs, education, and opportunity attracted the rural population to the cities, where religious groups practiced voluntary apartheid (segregation), separating themselves by religious sect to live in Christian or Muslim districts. There, they divided themselves further, separating themselves by sect. Shiites and Sunnis, both Muslim, largely lived in separate sectors of the city.

Failure of the Confessional System

It was apparent that Lebanon's confessional political system was not working. The final break of peaceful relations between Christians and Muslims occurred in April 1975. A group of gun-toting assassins made a failed attempt to kill Pierre Jumayyil, the leader of the Phalangist Movement, a

In the years preceding the civil war, Lebanon had become an international destination for the intelligentsia and the world-weary. Beirut was known as the Monaco of the Middle East. Books and publications, politics, and culture were discussed energetically, and music and poetry were abundant. The Lebanese people, renowned for their hospitality and sense of humor, entertained a continuous stream of foreign tourists, writers, and other scholarly visitors eager to savor in the city's many delights.

MEDITERRANEAN SEA

Sidon

ISRAEL

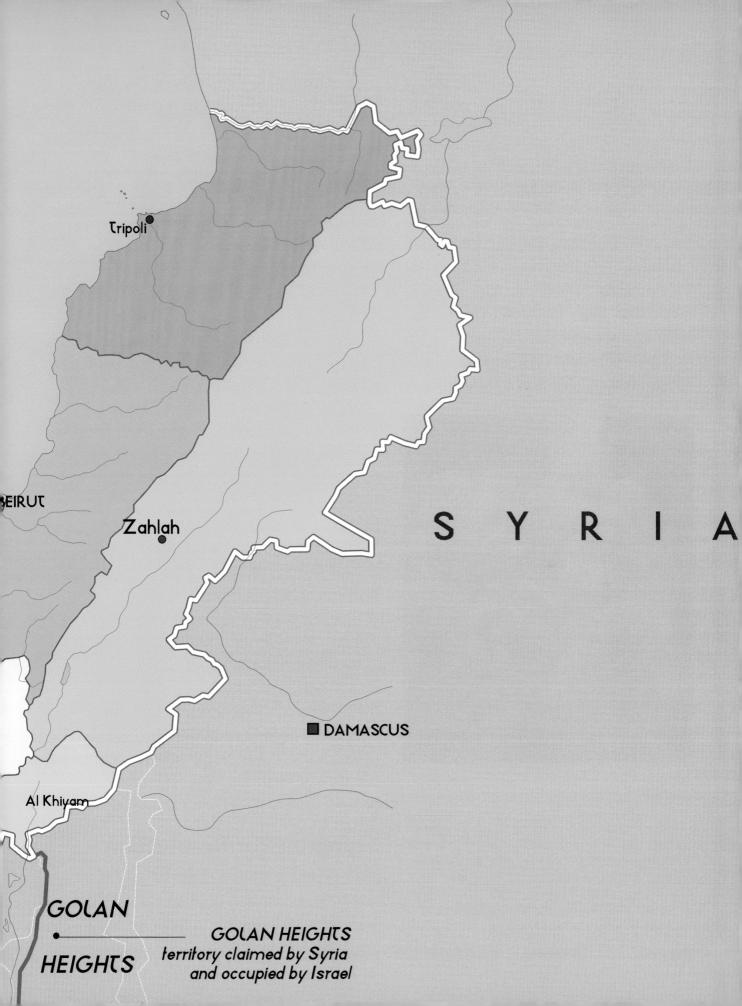

Tripoli

BEIRUT

Zahlah

S Y R I A

■ DAMASCUS

Al Khiyam

GOLAN

● ───────────

HEIGHTS

GOLAN HEIGHTS
territory claimed by Syria
and occupied by Israel

Christian (Israeli-supported) militia group. Although they did not succeed, they did manage to murder four of Jumayyil's companions. Believing that Palestinian guerrillas were behind this assassination attempt, the opposition retaliated by attacking a bus carrying Palestinians through a Christian neighborhood. Twenty-six Palestinians died in the attack, increasing the violence during the civil war in Lebanon.

The 1975–1976 civil war was seen as a failure of Lebanon's government,

Militiamen duck behind a barricade in Beirut during Lebanon's civil war period (1975–1991) in this 1975 photograph. Historians have estimated that at least 100,000 Lebanese died in the fighting that escalated during the long and bloody conflict between Christians and Muslims. Nearly 17,000 people remain without details about the fate of missing loved ones. Today, the Taif Agreement allows equal representation in the Lebanese Parliament between religious groups.

a confessional system where the loyalty of the people was to a particular religious sect, rather than to the nation as a whole. Adding to the turmoil was the Muslim belief that their population had substantially increased since 1932. Muslims now considered themselves a majority in Lebanon. The Christian Maronites, however, refused to share power. There was no agreement as to whether or not the army, thought to be pro-Christian, should be called out to help stop the fighting.

After a series of skirmishes in 1976, the Lebanese Front—which included Christian militia—faced the Palestine Liberation Organization (PLO) in battle when they began to attack Palestinian refugee camps. Syria was alarmed and feared that the fighting would spread to its borders. This prompted Syria's leaders to negotiate a seventeen-point peace agreement known as the Constitutional Document. This pact was short-lived and then completely disintegrated. Just after it had been decided upon, several Muslim army officers defected from their regiments and attacked the presidential palace.

Searching for Resolutions

One possible solution to Lebanon's fighting was the creation of two separate states—one Christian and

Prior to 1990, the constitution mandated that the president of Lebanon be chosen from the most populous religious sect. Based on a census taken in 1932, this mandate dictated that a Maronite Christian be chosen as president. This caused a great deal of contention and angered the many Muslims who felt that Christians no longer comprised the majority of Lebanon's populace. Under the constitutional reforms of 1990, a half-Christian, half-Muslim cabinet took over many of the powers of the Christian president. This change alleviated a great deal of the contention. Representatives from each of the country's religious groups govern present-day Lebanon, shown on this 2002 map.

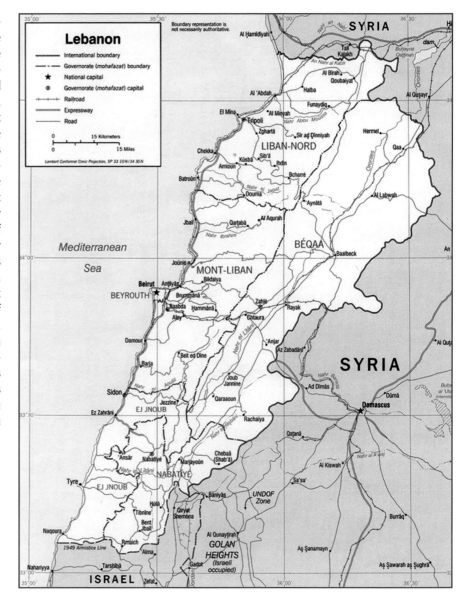

one Muslim. Before this could be resolved, however, Syria intervened militarily and broke the opposition. In October 1976, at an Arab League meeting and Riyadh Peace Conference in Cairo, the 1975–1976 Lebanese civil war was finally over. Casualties were estimated at nearly 44,000, with thousands of others displaced. A mostly Syrian military contingent called the Arab Deterrent Force (ADF) was dispatched to Lebanon to keep the peace, though fighting continued. Beirut, now divided into Muslim and Christian sections (and separated by the so-called Green Line) lay in shambles.

Destruction of the country's infrastructure during the war had tarnished the reputation that Lebanese-made products had once enjoyed. Now illegal, underground businesses imported inexpensive foreign goods and exported them with labels that claimed they were "Made in Lebanon."

After the civil war, there was often very little co-operation between the Lebanese government and the Syrian peacekeepers. The Lebanese army was in disarray and, in the south, the PLO had taken control. Syria was also conflicted between taking control of both the Christian and the Muslim factions and just leaving the Muslims to their own devices.

The standoff between the administration led by Lebanese president Elias Sarkis and Syrian control finally broke down. The ADF launched an all-out attack on Christian-controlled areas. In 1978, there was a UN-brokered cease-fire. However, uneasy relations between the two nations continued. To further inflame the situation, the Israel Defense

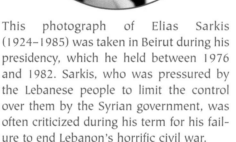

This photograph of Elias Sarkis (1924–1985) was taken in Beirut during his presidency, which he held between 1976 and 1982. Sarkis, who was pressured by the Lebanese people to limit the control over them by the Syrian government, was often criticized during his term for his failure to end Lebanon's horrific civil war.

Forces (IDF) and the South Lebanon Army (SLA) joined the fray. There were continuous clashes in Beirut, southern Lebanon, and elsewhere.

Industrial production slowed. Oil production was stopped, raising international prices. Raw materials from abroad became too expensive to import. Lebanon's economy was in shambles.

On October 23, 1983, a suicide bomber hit U.S. Marine barracks in Beirut, killing 241 Americans. Afterward, the United States suspended all financial assistance to Lebanon; however, the government was still able to secure assistance from Europe.

The international business community abandoned Lebanon when it saw no end to the sectarian fighting. Foreign banks, central to economic recovery in the region, began to close. The instability of the government and economy seemed to mean that Lebanon could never recover.

This photograph, taken during the Lebanese civil war in 1983, shows smoke billowing over Druze-controlled Tripoli during fighting between the Palestine Liberation Organization, Israeli forces, and Lebanese Druze and Christians. About one month earlier, the United States and Saudi governments helped organize a cease-fire agreement between Lebanon's Druze and Christian populations. The PLO-sponsored explosion was most likely a response to Israeli-led attacks in the region and the push by the United States for the PLO to leave the region in 1982.

Lebanon was now considered an outlaw nation. Domestic kidnappings numbered in the thousands.

There are essentially two economies in Lebanon. First there are the largely feudalistic, extremely impoverished rural areas, where the inhabitants use ancient, inefficient methods of farming and production. This is contrasted with urban areas consisting of a more sophisticated and educated population, which is separated into sectors of the city according to religious affiliation. There is no central factor to hold these diverse groups together.

Recovery

The 1975–1991 civil war period was disastrous for Lebanon. It ruined its infrastructure and damaged its economy, causing the nation to lose its place as the banking center for the Arab world. After peace was achieved in 1991, the government began to restore order. Small manufacturers reemerged, again producing goods and services. Internal stability, coupled with international assistance, enabled Lebanon to begin its recovery.

In 1993, the government began a program called Horizon 2000, a $20 billion reconstruction program. Inflation began to slow and production made solid gains. Lebanon has been successful at the reconstruction of its economy and the rebuilding of its war-torn cities. Business has since returned to Beirut.

Nevertheless, Lebanon continuously faces challenges, while suffering from religious-, political-, and ethnic-based turmoil. There is hope that in the future a permanent peace will be achieved for all the nations of the Middle East of which Lebanon is an integral part.

TIMELINE

3000 BC: First settlements of the Phoenicians

2000 BC: Invasion by the Amorites, coming from the east

1800 BC: Phoenician city-states become vassals under Egypt

1100 BC: Egypt loses its control over Phoenicia

539 BC: Phoenicia is conquered by Persia

333 BC: Phoenicia is conquered by Alexander the Great

AD 64: Lebanon is conquered by Rome and governed as part of Syria

637-639: Arab conquest and rule from Damascus

1098: The first crusader kingdom is established

1197: A slow Muslim reconquest begins

1289: Lebanon is controlled by the Egyptian Mamluks

1516: Ottomans take control over Lebanon

1697: Shihabs takes over the local power of Lebanon

1858: A civil war with many parties results in horrific bloodshed

1860: Civil war ends, with the Druze in a dominant position

1914–1918: World War I

1920: Lebanon is governed under a French mandate

1926: Lebanon's government is divided between Muslim and Christian leaders

1941: Joint occupation in Lebanon by British and free French forces

1943: French government recognizes Lebanese independence

1945: Lebanon joins the Arab League of States and the United Nations

1946: Real independence for Lebanon, after the last French troops have left

1948: Influx of Palestinians after war of Palestine and the establishment of Israel

1949: A coup promoting union with Syria fails

1950: Increase in Muslim opposition towards the government

1958: Short civil war ends with U.S. intervention

1961: A new coup promoting union with Syria fails

1975: Civil war starts, with Muslims against Maronite Christians (Phalange)

1976: PLO joins the Muslims with Syria, who were afraid of reactions from Israel

1978: Israeli invasion of Lebanon

1982: Israel invades again; U.S. forces PLO out; Christian president Bashir is killed

1985: Heavy fighting over southern Lebanon starts after withdrawal of Israeli troops

1989: Lebanon issues a new constitution allowing more Muslims power

1990: Lebanese troops defeated by Syrian army; Lebanese president Aoun
   is exiled

1992: Elections for Lebanon's new National Assembly

1996: Hizbullah wins eight seats in National Assembly; Israeli attack in Beirut

1997: Fighting between Hizbullah and Israeli forces; Lahoud elected new president

1998: The Lebanese government continues rebuilding after civil war damage

2000: Israeli troops withdraw from southern Lebanon

2001: Lebanese demand withdrawal of Syrian military

2002: Lebanese demand control over Israeli-occupied Golan Heights

2003: Lebanese prime minister Rafiq Hariri discusses his concerns with French
   prime minister Jacques Chirac over possible U.S. war with Iraq

GLOSSARY

Asia Minor The peninsula forming the western extremity of Asia between the Black Sea in the north, the Mediterranean Sea in the south, and the Aegean Sea in the west.

bedouin A nomadic Arab of the Arabian, Syrian, or North African deserts.

caliph A successor of Muhammad as temporal and spiritual head of Islam.

Canaanite A member of a Semitic people inhabiting ancient Palestine and Phoenicia from about 3000 BC.

cedar Any of a genus of usually tall coniferous trees of the pine family noted for their fragrant and durable wood.

Christian One who professes belief in the teachings of Jesus Christ.

confessional state A state organized according to religious affiliation.

Druze Religious community originating in Egypt that is generally considered Muslim but whose practices also contain elements of Christianity.

Eisenhower Doctrine An agreement from January 1957 that offered U.S. economic and military aid to Middle Eastern countries to counteract Soviet influence in the region.

feudalistic An adjective describing a system of political organization in which lands are not privately owned by citizens, but by the state. Citizens may be granted the right to farm those same lands, but usually through an agreement with the state.

Greater Syria Term used by historians to designate the region that includes the present-day states of Jordan, Israel, Lebanon, and Syria.

Green Line A no-man's-land created in Beirut during the 1975 civil war by the forward lines of advance of each contending force. This line separated Christian East Beirut from Muslim West Beirut.

hermitage A secluded residence or private retreat.

Islam The religious faith of Muslims including belief in Allah as the sole deity and in Muhammad as his prophet.

jihad A holy war that is fought by Muslims against people who are a threat to the Islamic religion or who oppose its teachings.

Koran The book composed of writings accepted by Muslims as revelations made to Muhammad by Allah through the angel Gabriel.

mandate The authority given to an elected group of people, such as a government, to perform an action or govern a country.

Maronites The largest Christian sect in Lebanon, which settled there in the mid-seventh century. Maronites continue to live in sections of the nation, especially in East Beirut.

martyr A person who is put to death for adhering to a belief, faith, or profession.

Muslim A worshiper of Islam.

nationalism The desire for and the attempt to achieve political independence for one's country.

Phoenician A native or inhabitant of ancient Phoenicia.

sectarian Belonging and adhering to a specific sect or division.

Semite A member of any group of peoples of southwestern Asia, chiefly represented now by the Jews and Arabs but in ancient times also by the Babylonians, Assyrians, Aramaeans, Canaanites, and Phoenicians.

Semitic Relating to, or characteristic of, the Semites.

FOR MORE INFORMATION

American-Arab Anti-Discrimination
    Committee
4201 Connecticut Avenue
Washington, DC 20008
(202) 244-2990
e-mail: adc@adc.org
Web site: http://www.adc.org

Center for Middle Eastern Studies
The University of Texas at Austin
One University Station, #F9400
Austin, TX 78712-1193
(512) 471-3881
e-mail: cmes@menic.utexas.edu
Web site:
    http://menic.utexas.edu/menic

Foundation for Middle East Peace
    (FMEP)
1761 N Street NW
Washington, DC 20036
(202) 835-3650
e-mail: pcwilcox@fmep.org
Web site: http://www.fmep.org

Web Sites

Due to the changing nature of Internet
link, the Rosen Publishing Group, Inc.,
has developed an online list of Web
sites related to the subject of this book.
The site is updated regularly. Please
use this link to access the list:

http://www.rosenlinks.com/liha/leba

FOR FURTHER READING

Eshel, Issac. *Lebanon in Pictures*
    (Visual Geography Series).
    Minneapolis: Lerner Publications
    Company, 1992.
Hutchison, Linda. *Lebanon* (Modern
    Nations of the World). San Diego:
    Lucent Books, 2003.

McDaniel, Jan. *Lebanon* (Modern Middle
    Eastern Nations and Their Strategic
    Place in the World). Brookshire, TX:
    Mason Crest Publishers, 2003.
Sheehan, Sean. *Lebanon* (Cultures of the
    World). New York: Benchmark
    Books, 1997.

BIBLIOGRAPHY

Cobban, Helena. *The Making of Modern
    Lebanon*. Boulder, CO: Westview
    Press, 1985.
Evans, Louella. *Portrait of a People:
    Lebanon*. New York: Graphic
    Society, 1972.
Gilmour, David. *Lebanon: The Fractured
    Country*. New York: St. Martin's
    Press, 1983.
Gordon, David. *The Republic of
    Lebanon*. Boulder, CO: Westview
    Press, 1983.
Hitti, Philip. *A Short History of Lebanon*.
    New York: St. Martin's Press, 1965.

Hyper-History Online. "The Historical
    Origins of Islam." Retrieved July 10,
    2002 (http://hyperhistory.com).
Jansen, Michael. *The Battle of Beirut*.
    Boston: South End Press, 1983.
Library of Congress. "Lebanon, A
    Country Study." Retrieved May 15,
    2002 (http://www.infoplease.com).
Mackey, Sandra. *Death of a Nation*. New
    York: Congdon & Weed, Inc., 1989.
Petran, Tabitha. *The Struggle over
    Lebanon*. New York: Monthly
    Review Press, 1987.

INDEX

About the Author

Carolyn M. Skahill is a freelance writer living in West Hartford, Connecticut. She holds an MA in economics as well as an MBA and is employed in the financial communications business at a public company.

Acknowledgments

Special thanks to Karin van der Tak for her expert guidance regarding matters pertaining to the Middle East and Asia.

Photo Credits

Cover (map) , pp. 1 (foreground), 4–5, 54–55 © 2002 Geoatlas; cover (background), pp. 1 (background), 16–17, 18–19, 26, 28–29, 39, 41 (inset), 57 Courtesy of the General Libraries, The University of Texas at Austin; cover (top left) © AP/Wide World Photos; cover (bottom left), cover (bottom right), p. 37 © The Art Archive/Topkapi Museum Istanbul/ Dagli Orti; pp. 6, 51 © AFP/Corbis; pp. 8, 9, 12–13, 20, 22–23, 40–41, 44, 46–47, 52 Maps designed by Tahara Hasan; p. 11 © The British Library; p. 14 © Sonia Halliday Photographs/F.H.C. Birch; pp. 17, 18 (inset), 37 © Sonia Halliday Photographs; p. 21 © AKG London/Erich Lessing; pp. 24, 32 © AKG London; p. 30 © Archivo Iconografico, S.A./Corbis; pp. 34–35 © Historical Picture Archive/Corbis; p. 38 © Charles and Josette Lenars/Corbis; p. 43 © Underwood and Underwood/Corbis; p. 48 © Hulton-Deutsch Collection/Corbis; pp. 50, 58 © Bettmann/ Corbis; p. 53 © David Rubinger/Corbis; p. 56 © Hulton/Archive/Getty Images; p. 59 © Francoise de Mulder/Corbis.

Designer: Tahara Hasan; **Editor:** Joann Jovinelly; **Photo Researcher:** Elizabeth Loving